Piano • Vocal • Guitar

THE MISEDUCATION OF LAURYN HILL

Contents

ISBN 0-634-00245-7

HAL•LEONARD®
CORPORATION
7777 W. BLUEMOUND RD. P.O. BOX 13819 MILWAUKEE, WI 53213

For all works contained herein:
Unauthorized copying, arranging, adapting, recording or public performance is an infringement of copyright.
Infringers are liable under the law.

Visit Hal Leonard Online at
www.halleonard.com

Lost Ones

Written by LAURYN HILL
and FREDERICK HIBBERT

Copyright © 1998 Sony/ATV Tunes LLC, Obverse Creation Music and Songs Of PolyGram International, Inc.
All Rights on behalf of Sony/ATV Tunes LLC and Obverse Creation Music
Administered by Sony/ATV Music Publishing, 8 Music Square West, Nashville, TN 37203
International Copyright Secured   All Rights Reserved
- contains elements from "Bam Bam" by Frederick Hibbert, published by Songs Of PolyGram International, Inc.

CHORUS 2

You might win some but you just lost one. You might win some but you just lost one. You

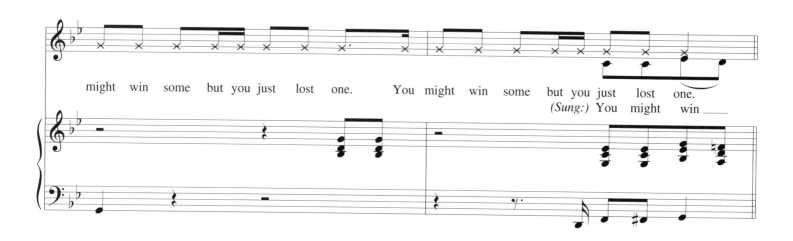

might win some but you just lost one. You might win some but you just lost one. You
(Sung:) You might win ____

some but you real-ly lost one. ____ You just lost ____ one, it's so sil-ly how

come. ____ When it's all ____ done, did you real-ly gain from? ____ What you done ____

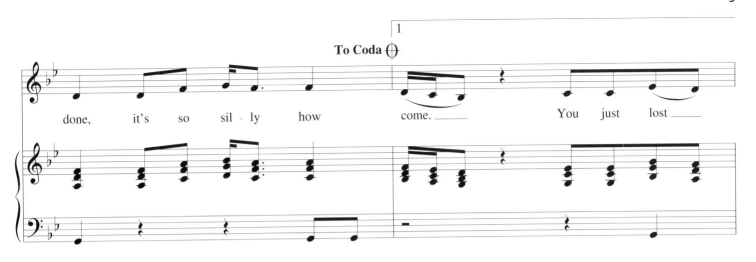

To Coda

done, it's so sil - ly how come. _____ You just lost _____

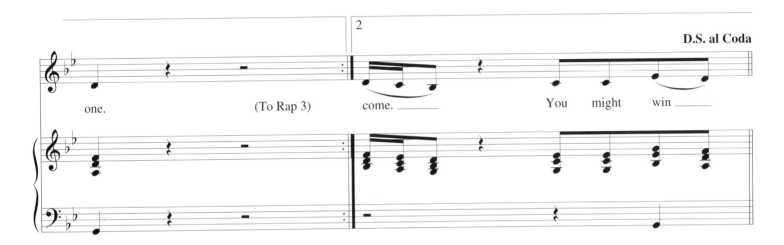

D.S. al Coda

one. (To Rap 3) come. _____ You might win _____

CODA

Play 7 times

come _____ You just lost _____ one. You just lost _____

one. What's a bum _____ bum?

Rap Lyrics

Rap 1: It's funny how money change a situation.
(Loop 1) Miscommunication leads to complication.
My emancipation don't fit your equation.
I was on the humble, you—on every station.
Some wan' play young Lauryn like she dumb.
But remember not a game new under the sun.
Everything you did has already been done.
I know all the tricks from Bricks to Kingston.
My ting done made your kingdom wan' run.
Now understand L. Boogie's non-violent.
But if a thing test me, run for mi gun.
Can't take a threat to mi newborn son.
L's been this way since creation.
A groupie call, you fall from temptation.
Now you wanna ball over separation.
Tarnish my image in your conversation.
Who you gon' scrimmage, like you the champion.
You might win some but you just lost one.

Chorus 1:

Rap 2: Now, now how come your talk turn cold?
(Loop 2) Gained the whole world for the price of your soul.
Tryin' to grab hold of what you can't control.
Now you're all floss, what a sight to behold.
Wisdom is better than silver and gold.
I was hopeless now I'm on Hope road.
Every man want to act like he's exempt
When him need to get down on his knees and repent.
Can't slick talk on the day of judgment.
Your movement's similar to a serpent.
Tried to play straight, how your whole style bent?
Consequence is no coincidence.
Hypocrites always want to play innocent.
Always want to take it to the full out extent.
Always want to make it seem like good intent.
Never want to face it when it's time for punishment.
I know that you don't wanna hear my opinion.
But there come many paths and you must choose one.
And if you don't change then the rain soon come.
See you might win some but you just lost one.

Chorus 2:

Rap 3: Now don't you understand man universal law.
(Loop 2) What you throw out comes back to you, star.
Never underestimate those who you scar.
'Cause karma, karma, karma comes back to you hard.
You can't hold God's people back that long.
The chain of Shatan wasn't made that strong.
Trying to pretend like your word is your bond.
But until you do right, all you do will go wrong.
Now some might mistake this for just a simple song.
And some don't know what they have 'til it's gone.
Now even when you're gone you can still be reborn.
And, from the night can arrive the sweet dawn.
Now, some might listen and some might shun.
And some may think that they've reached perfection.
If you look closely you'll see what you've become.
'Cause you might win some but you just lost one.

Repeat Chorus 2:
(with D.S.)

Ex-Factor

Written by LAURYN HILL, GARY GRICE,
CLIFFORD SMITH, COREY WOODS, DENNIS COLES,
JASON HUNTER, LAMONT HAWKINS, ROBERT DIGGS JR.,
RUSSELL JONES, ALAN BERGMAN, MARILYN BERGMAN and MARVIN HAMLISCH

It could all be so sim - ple.
Is this just a sil - ly game
I keep let - ting you back in.

But you'd rath - er make it hard.
that forc - es you to act this way?
How can I ex - plain my - self?

Original key: F# major. This edition has been transposed down one half-step to be more playable.

Copyright © 1998 Sony/ATV Tunes LLC, Obverse Creation Music, BMG Songs, Inc.,
Careers-BMG Music Publishing, Inc., Wu-Tang Publishing and Colgems-EMI Music Inc.
All Rights on behalf of Sony/ATV Tunes LLC and Obverse Creation Music Administered by Sony/ATV Music Publishing, 8 Music Square West, Nashville, TN 37203
All Rights on behalf of Wu-Tang Publishing Administered by Careers-BMG Music Publishing, Inc.
International Copyright Secured   All Rights Reserved
- contains elements from "Can It All Be So Simple" by Alan Bergman, Marilyn Bergman, Marvin Hamlisch,
Robert Diggs Jr., Dennis Coles, Gary Grice, Corey Woods, Lamont Hawkins, Clifford Smith, Russell Jones and Jason Hunter
- "Can It All Be So Simple" contains elements of "The Way We Were" by Alan Bergman, Marilyn Bergman and Marvin Hamlisch

To Zion

Written by LAURYN HILL,
CHARLES FOX and NORMAN GIMBEL

Steadily, not fast

Un - sure what the bal - ance held, _ I touched _ my
How beau - ti - ful if noth - ing more _ than ___ to

*Written one octave higher than sung

Copyright © 1998 Sony/ATV Tunes LLC, Obverse Creation Music, Rodali Music and Fox/Gimbel Productions, Inc.
All Rights on behalf of Sony/ATV Tunes LLC, Obverse Creation Music and Rodali Music
Administered by Sony/ATV Music Publishing, 8 Music Square West, Nashville, TN 37203
International Copyright Secured All Rights Reserved
- contains elements from "And The Feeling's Good" by Charles Fox and Norman Gimbel,
published by Rodali Music (administered by Sony/ATV Music Publishing) and Fox/Gimbel Productions, Inc.

Zi - on, beau - ti - ful, beau - ti - ful Zi - on. March - ing, march - ing to

Zi - on, beau - ti - ful, beau - ti - ful Zi - on. Beau - ti - ful, beau - ti - ful

Zi - on, beau - ti - ful, beau - ti - ful Zi - on. Beau - ti - ful, beau - ti - ful

Zi - on, beau - ti - ful, beau - ti - ful Zi - on. Beau - ti - ful, beau - ti - ful Zi - on. ____

Doo Wop
(That Thing)

Written by
LAURYN HILL

Copyright © 1998 Sony/ATV Tunes LLC and Obverse Creation Music
All Rights Administered by Sony/ATV Music Publishing, 8 Music Square West, Nashville, TN 37203
International Copyright Secured   All Rights Reserved

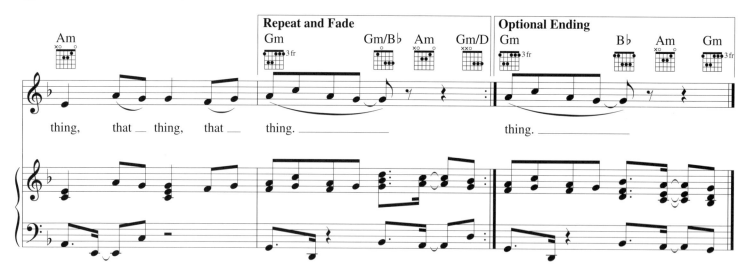

thing,   that __ thing,   that __ thing. _____   thing. _____

Additional Lyrics

Rap 1:   It's been three weeks since you've been lookin' for your friend,
The one you let hit it and never called you again.
'Member when he told you he was 'bout the Benjamins.
You act like you ain't hear him, then give 'em a little trim.
To begin, how you think you really gon' pretend?
Like you wasn't down, then you called him again.

Plus when, you give it up so easy you ain't even foolin' him.
If you did it then, then you probably fuck again.
Talkin' out your neck sayin' you're a Christian,
A Muslim sleepin' wit' the gin.
Now that was the sin that did Jezabel in.
Who you gon' tell when repercussion spin?

Showin' off your ass 'cause you're thinkin' it's a trend.
Girlfriend, let me break it down for you again.
You know I only say it 'cause I'm truly genuine.
Don't be a hard rock when you really a gem.
Baby girl, respect is just the minimum.
Niggas fucked up and you still defendin' 'em.

Now, Lauryn is only human.
Don't think I haven't been through the same predicament.
Let it sit inside your head like a million in Philly Penn.
It's silly when girls sell their souls because it's in. Look at where you bein.
Hair weaves like Europeans, fake nails done by Koreans.

Rap 2:   The second verse is dedicated to the men
More concerned wit' his rims and his timbs than his women.
Him and his men come in the cub like hooligans.
Don't care who they defend, popping Yang like you got yen.

Let's not pretend,
They wanna pack pistol by they waist men.
Cristal by the case men, still they in they mother's basement.
The pretty face men claimin' that they did a bid men.
Need to take care of their three and four kids, men.

They facin' court case when the child support's late.
Money takin', heart breakin. Now you wonder why women hate men.
And the sneaky, silent men, the punk domestic violence men.
The quick to shoot the semen stop actin' like boys and be men.

How you gon' win when you ain't right within? *(3x's)*
Uh-uh, come again.

Superstar

Written by LAURYN HILL
With Additional Lyrical Contribution
by JOHARI NEWTON and Additional Musical
Contribution by JAMES POYSER

Steadily

(Spoken:) Yo, hip-hop started out in the heart, uh-huh, yo. Now everybody tryin' to chart. Say what?

Hip-hop started out in the heart, yo, uh. Now everybody tryin' to chart. C'-mon

now, ba-by. C'-mon now, ba-by. C'-mon now, ba-by. C'-mon. Woo. C'-mon

Copyright © 1998 Sony/ATV Tunes LLC, Obverse Creation Music and Jermaine Music
All Rights Administered by Sony/ATV Music Publishing, 8 Music Square West, Nashville, TN 37203
International Copyright Secured   All Rights Reserved
- contains elements from "Light My Fire" by The Doors, published by Doors Music Co.

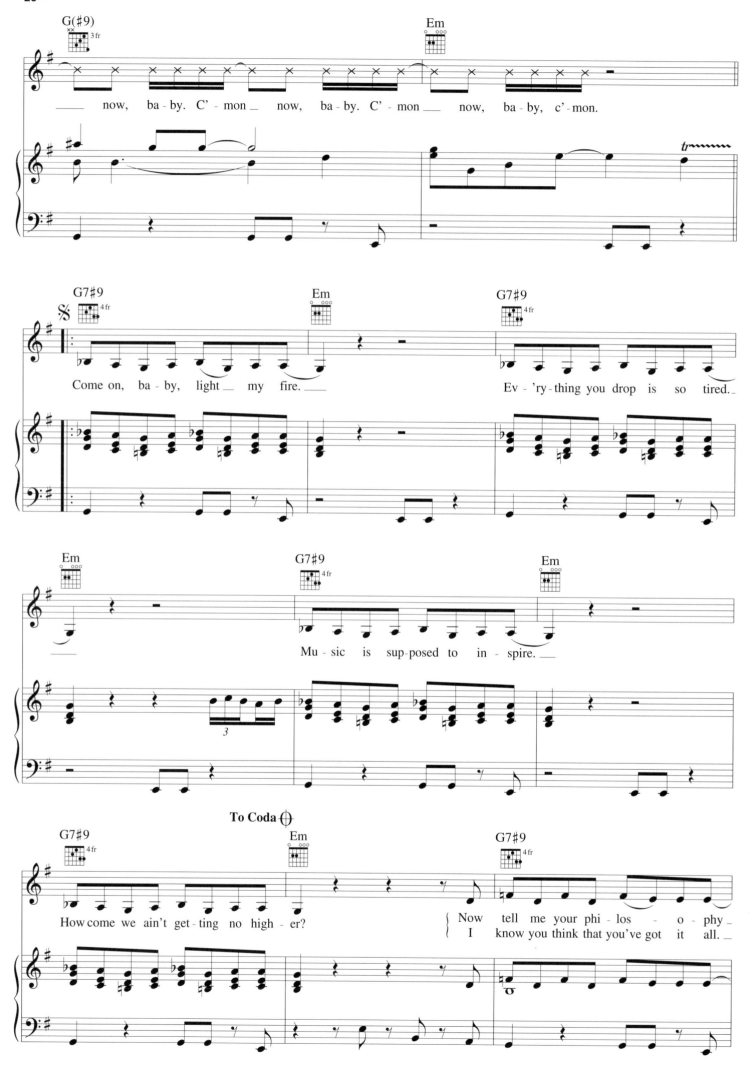

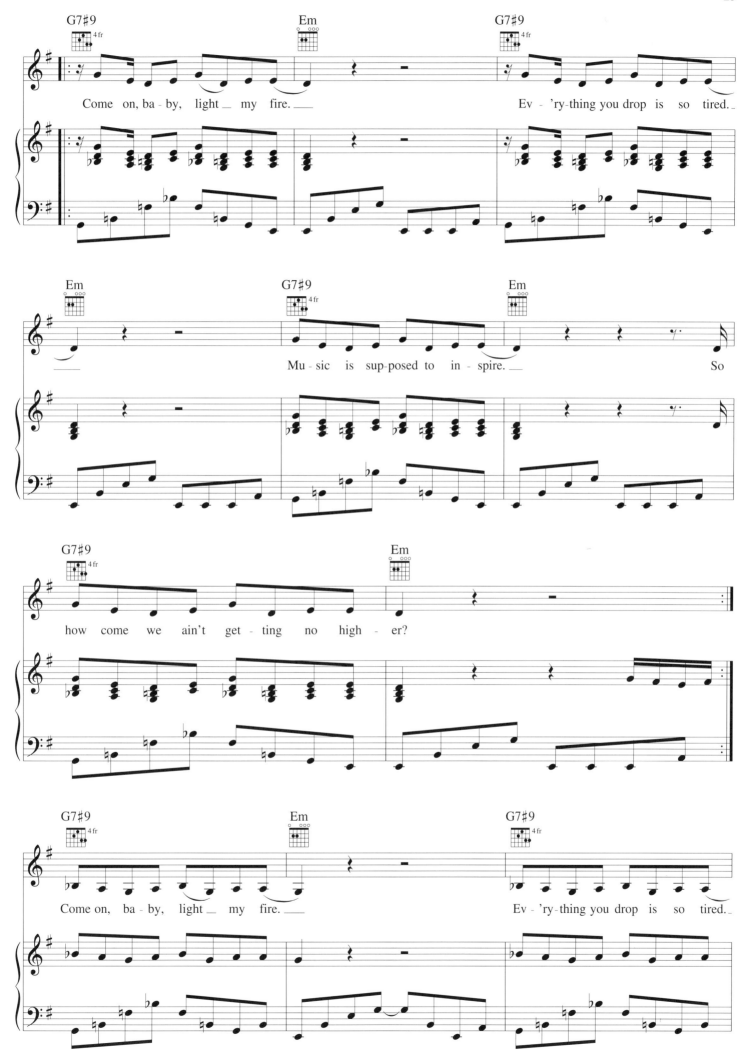

Additional Lyrics

Rap: I cross sands in distant lands, made plans with the sheiks.
Why you beef with freaks as my album sales peak?
All I wanted was to sell like 500
And be a ghetto superstar since my first album, *Blunted.*
I used to work at Foot Locker, they fired me and fronted.
Or I quitted, now I spit it—however do you want it?
Now you get it!
Writing rhymes my range with the frames slightly tinted.
Then send it to your block and have my full name cemented.
And if your rhymes sound like mine, I'm taking a percentage.
Unprecedented and still respected when it vintage.
I'm serious, I'm taking over areas in Aquarius.
Running red lights with my 10,000 chariots.
Just as Christ was a superstar, you stupid star.
They'll hail you then they'll nail you, no matter who you are.
They'll make you now then take you down.
And make you face it, if you slit the bag open.
And put your pinky in it, then taste it.

Final Hour

Written by LAURYN HILL
and DJ PREMIER

(Spoken:) Like fungus among us.

Rap 1-3: (See Rap lyrics)

Copyright © 1998 Sony/ATV Tunes LLC, Obverse Creation Music and DJ Premier Publishing Designee
All Rights on behalf of Sony/ATV Tunes LLC and Obverse Creation Music
Administered by Sony/ATV Music Publishing, 8 Music Square West, Nashville, TN 37203
International Copyright Secured   All Rights Reserved

CHORUS 1

You can get the mon-ey. You can get the pow-er. But keep your eyes on the fi-nal ho-ur.

You can get the mon-ey. You can get the pow-er. But keep your eyes on the fi-nal ho-ur.

CHORUS 2

(Sung:) You could get the mon — ey _____ and __ you could get the
(Spoken:) You can get the money. You can get the power. Keep your eyes on the final hour.

pow - er. _____
You can get the money. You can get the power. But keep your eyes on the final hour.

ENDING

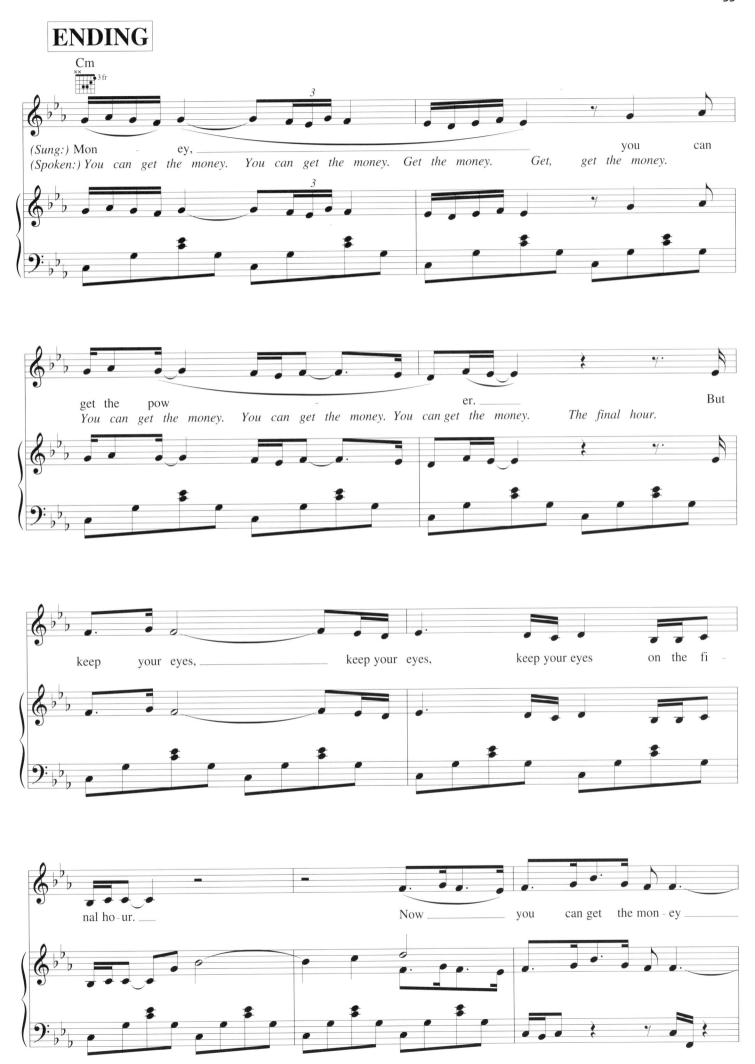

Rap Lyrics

Rap 1: I treat this like my thesis.
(Loop 8x) Well-written topic
Broken down into pieces.
I introduce then produce
Words so profuse.
It's abuse how I juice up this beat
Like I'm deuce.
Two people both equal.
Like I'm Gemini
Rather simeon.
If I Jimmy on this lock I could pop it.
You can't stop it.
Drop it.
Your whole crew's microscopic
Like particles while I make international articles.
And on the cover
Don't discus the baby mother business.
I been in this third LP you can't tell me, I witness.
First handed I'm candid.
You can't stand it.
Respect demanded
And get flown around the planet.
Rock Hard like granite or steel.
People feel Lauryn Hill from New-Ark to Israel.
And this is real.
So I keep makin' the street's ballads
While you lookin' for dressin' to go with your tossed salad.

Chorus 1:

Rap 2: I'm about to change the focus
(Loop 7x) From the richest to the brokest.
I wrote this opus
To reverse the hypnosis.
Whoever's closest
To the line's gonna win it.
You gonna fall tryin' to ball
While my team win the pennant.
I'm about to be in it
For a minute.
Then run for the senate.
Make a slum lord be the tenant.
Give his money to kids to spend it.
And then amend it.
Every law that ever prevented.
Our survival since our arrival
Documented in The Bible.
Like Moses and Aaron.
Things gon change, it's apparent.
And all the transparent gonna
Be seen through.
Let God redeem you.
Keep your deen true.
You can get the green, too.
Watch out what you cling to.
Observe how a queen do.
And I remain calm readin' the 73 Psalm.
'Cause wit all this on I got the world in palm.

Chorus 2:

Rap 3: Now I be breakin' bread sippin
(Loop 8x) Manichevitz wine.
Pay no mind party like it's 1999.
But when it comes down to ground beef like Palestine.
Say your rhymes, lets see if that get you out your bend.
Now I'm a get the mozzarella like a Rockerfeller.
Still be in the church of Lalibela.
Singing hymns a cappella.
Whether posed in Maribella in Couture
Or collectin' residuals from off *The Score*.
I'm makin' sure
I'm with the 144.
I've been here before this ain't a battle this is war.
Word to Boonie
I makes a lot like a Sunni.
Get diplomatic immunity in every ghetto community.
Had opportunity went from
Hoodshock to Hood-chic.
But it ain't what you cop
It's about what you keep.
And even if there are leaks
You can't capsize this ship.
'Cause I baptize my lips every time I take a sip.

Chorus 1 (2x):
Ending:

When It Hurts So Bad

Written by
LAURYN HILL

Moderately slow

When it hurts so bad, _____ when it hurts so bad, _____ why's it feel _____

_____ so good? _____ When it hurts so bad, _____ when it hurts so

bad, _____ why's it feel _____ so good? _____

Copyright © 1998 Sony/ATV Tunes LLC and Obverse Creation Music
All Rights Administered by Sony/ATV Music Publishing, 8 Music Square West, Nashville, TN 37203
International Copyright Secured   All Rights Reserved

I Used To Love Him

Written by LAURYN HILL
and DJ ROGER

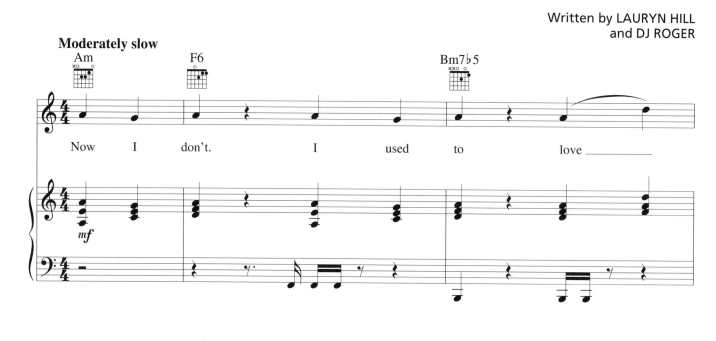

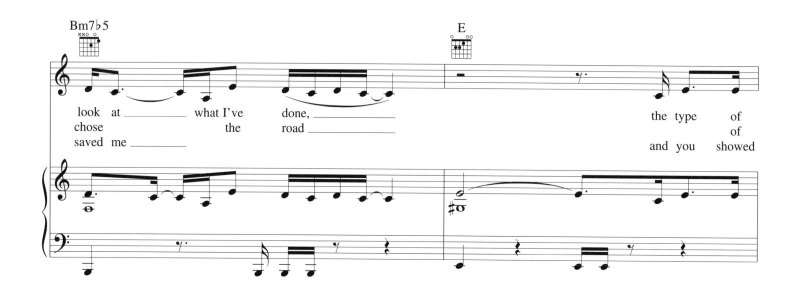

Copyright © 1998 Sony/ATV Tunes LLC, Obverse Creation Music and Soch Music
All Rights on behalf of Sony/ATV Tunes LLC and Obverse Creation Music Administered by
Sony/ATV Music Publishing, 8 Music Square West, Nashville, TN 37203
International Copyright Secured   All Rights Reserved

48

Forgive Them Father

Written by
LAURYN HILL

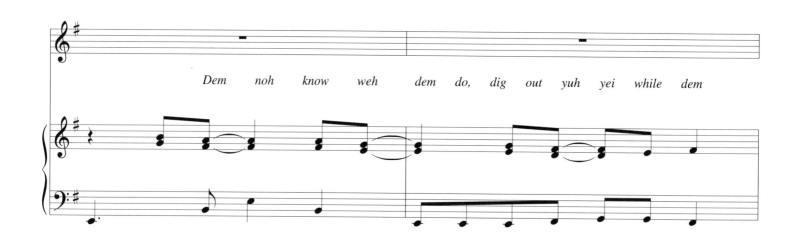

Copyright © 1998 Sony/ATV Tunes LLC and Obverse Creation Music
All Rights Administered by Sony/ATV Music Publishing, 8 Music Square West, Nashville, TN 37203
International Copyright Secured   All Rights Reserved

56

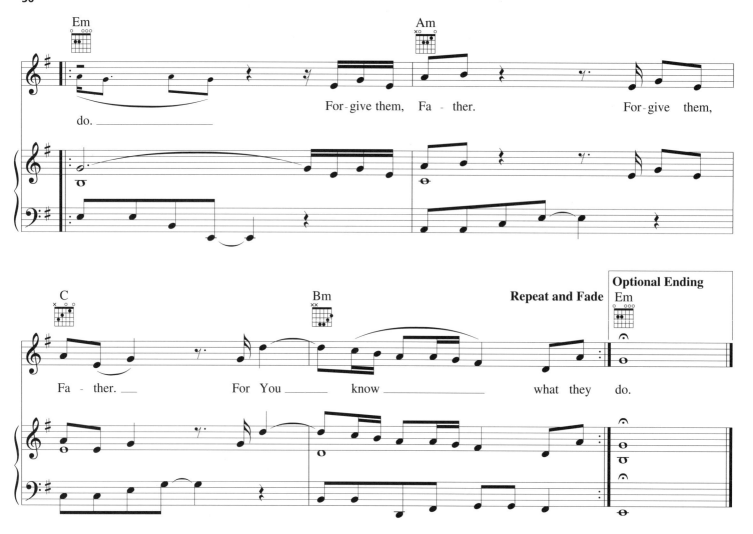

Additional Lyrics

Rap 1: Why every Indian wanna be the chief?
Feed a man 'til he's full and he still want beef.
Give me grief, try to tief off my piece.
Why for you to increase, I must decrease?
If I treat you kindly does it mean that I'm weak?
You hear me speak and think I won't take it to the streets.
I know enough cats that don't turn the other cheek.
But I try to keep it civilized like Menelik.
And other African czars observing stars with war scars.
Get yours in this capitalistic system.
So many caught or got bought you can't list them.
How you gonna idolize the missing?
To survive is to stay alive in the face of opposition.
Even when they comin' gunnin',
I stand position.
L's known the mission since conception.
Let's free the people from deception.
If you looking for the answers
Then you gotta ask the questions.
And when I let go, my voice echoes through the ghetto.
Sick of men trying to pull strings like Geppetto.
Why black people always be the ones to settle?
March through these streets like Soweto.

Rap 2: Gwan like dem love while dem rip yuh to shreds.
Trample pon yuh heart and lef yuh fi dead.
Dem a yuh fren who yuh depen pon from way back when.
But if yuh gi dem yuh back den yuh mus meet yuh end.
Dem noh know wey dem do.
Dem no know, dem no know, dem no know.
Dem no know, dem no know wey dem do.

Every Ghetto, Every City

Written by LAURYN HILL
and DAVID AXELROD

Copyright © 1998 Sony/ATV Tunes LLC, Obverse Creation Music and Scanian Music
All Rights on behalf of Sony/ATV Tunes LLC and Obverse Creation Music Administered by
Sony/ATV Music Publishing, 8 Music Square West, Nashville, TN 37203
International Copyright Secured   All Rights Reserved
- contains elements from "Tony Poem" by David Axelrod, published by Scanian Music
and "Jack Your Body" by S. Hurley, published by Silktone Songs, Inc. and Last Songs, Inc.

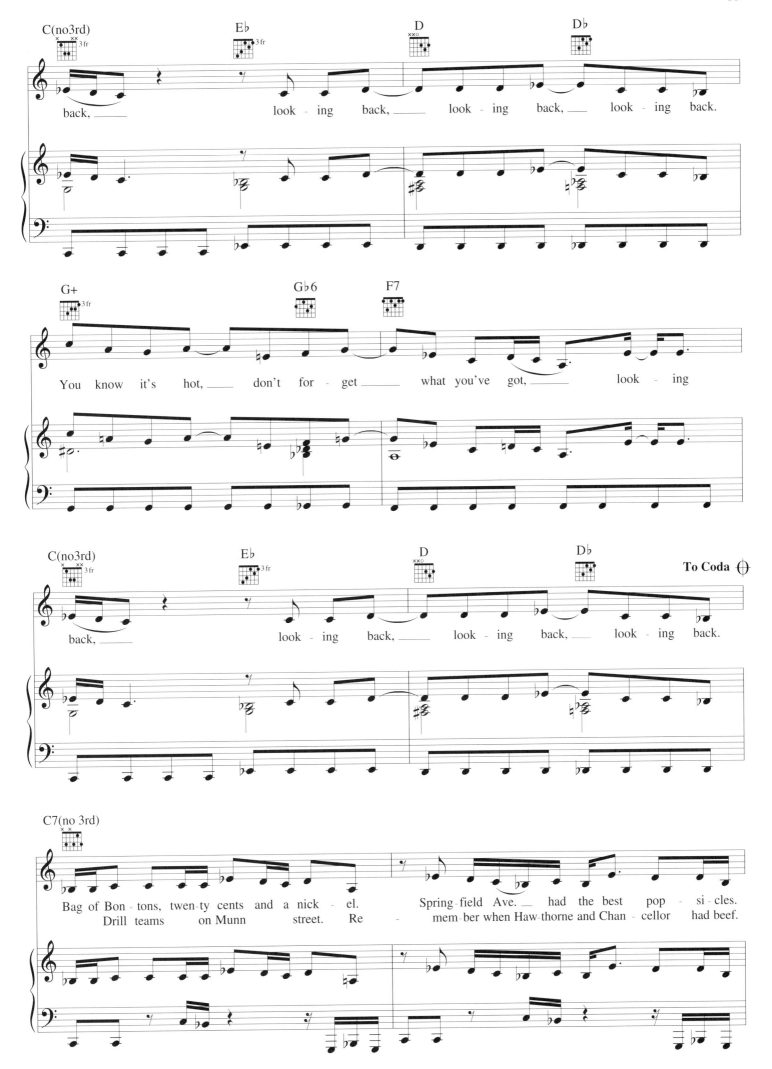

60

62

Nothing Even Matters

Written by
LAURYN HILL

Now the _____ skies _____ could fall, _____ not e - ven if my
could drift out to sea, _____ some nat - u - ral ca -
find me at no store, _____ I have no time for

* Vocal written an octave higher than sung

Copyright © 1998 Sony/ATV Tunes LLC and Obverse Creation Music
All Rights Administered by Sony/ATV Music Publishing, 8 Music Square West, Nashville, TN 37203
International Copyright Secured All Rights Reserved

66

Everything Is Everything

Written by LAURYN HILL
With Additional Lyrical Contribution
by JOHARI NEWTON

Copyright © 1998 Sony/ATV Tunes LLC, Obverse Creation Music and Jermaine Music
All Rights Administered by Sony/ATV Music Publishing, 8 Music Square West, Nashville, TN 37203
International Copyright Secured   All Rights Reserved

75

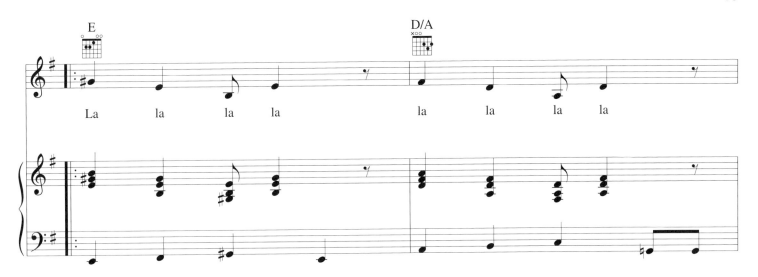

Additional Lyrics

Rap: I philosophy, possibly speaking tongues,
Beat drum, Abyssinian, street Baptist.
Rap this in fine linen from the beginning.

My practice extending across the atlas.
I begat this.
Flippin' in the ghetto on a dirty mattress.
You can't match this rapper/actress.
More powerful than two Cleopatras.
Bomb graffiti on the tomb of Nefertiti.
MCs ain't ready to take it to the Serengeti.
My rhymes is heavy like the mind of Sister Betty.
L. Boogie spars with stars and constellations.
Then came down for a little conversation.
Adjacent to the king, fear no human being.
Roll with cherubims to Nassau Coliseum.
Now hear this mixture where hip hop meets scripture.
Develop a negative into a positive picture.

The Miseducation Of Lauryn Hill

Written by LAURYN HILL
With Additional Musical Contribution
by TEJUNOLD NEWTON

Original key: E♭ minor

Copyright © 1998 Sony/ATV Tunes LLC, Obverse Creation Music and Jermaine Music
All Rights Administered by Sony/ATV Music Publishing, 8 Music Square West, Nashville, TN 37203
International Copyright Secured   All Rights Reserved